A Mantra A Day

Gabrielle B.

Copyright © 2020 Gabrielle B.
All rights reserved.

Cover design and illustrations
by Denique Nashay of SightofShe

Thank you to all who contributed to making this book what it is.
I love you. Enjoy.

MANTRA #1

Thank God for the day.
And for the one that may follow.
I release yesterday's cares.
I release yesterday's sorrow.
Because just like an eagle with wings I will soar.
And fully embrace whatever is in store.
Come sun.
Come clouds.
Come hail.
Come rain.
I will fully embrace whatever comes my way.

*List 3 things
that you are grateful for.*

MANTRA #2

Breathing in,
I release the pressure.
That I feel has been placed upon me.
Breathing out,
I increase the effort.
Let my blessings fall at my feet.

*What are you releasing
and what are you receiving?*

A DEEP BREATH

Me, just a spot in the sky.
Or, a spotlight.
A pure perspective is the potential of direction.
In which direction will you allow your emotions to travel?
In which election will you validate self-power?
In which inception will you appreciate each outcome?
At least there was an outcome.
In the proper form you can watch the storm look more like a message of raining blessings.
I've learned that a deep breath is a mental reset, had to press eject on societal presets.
Trust more and eat less.
The way to limit the access of light? Feel death.
Alone in a desert I was presented with this revelation, it was a deep test. I took a deep breath. And chose the path of least stress.

- Willis Lusk II

MANTRA #3

I relinquish control.
Over all I know.
I fully surrender to the unknown.

Will you choose the path of least resistance by surrendering to what is?

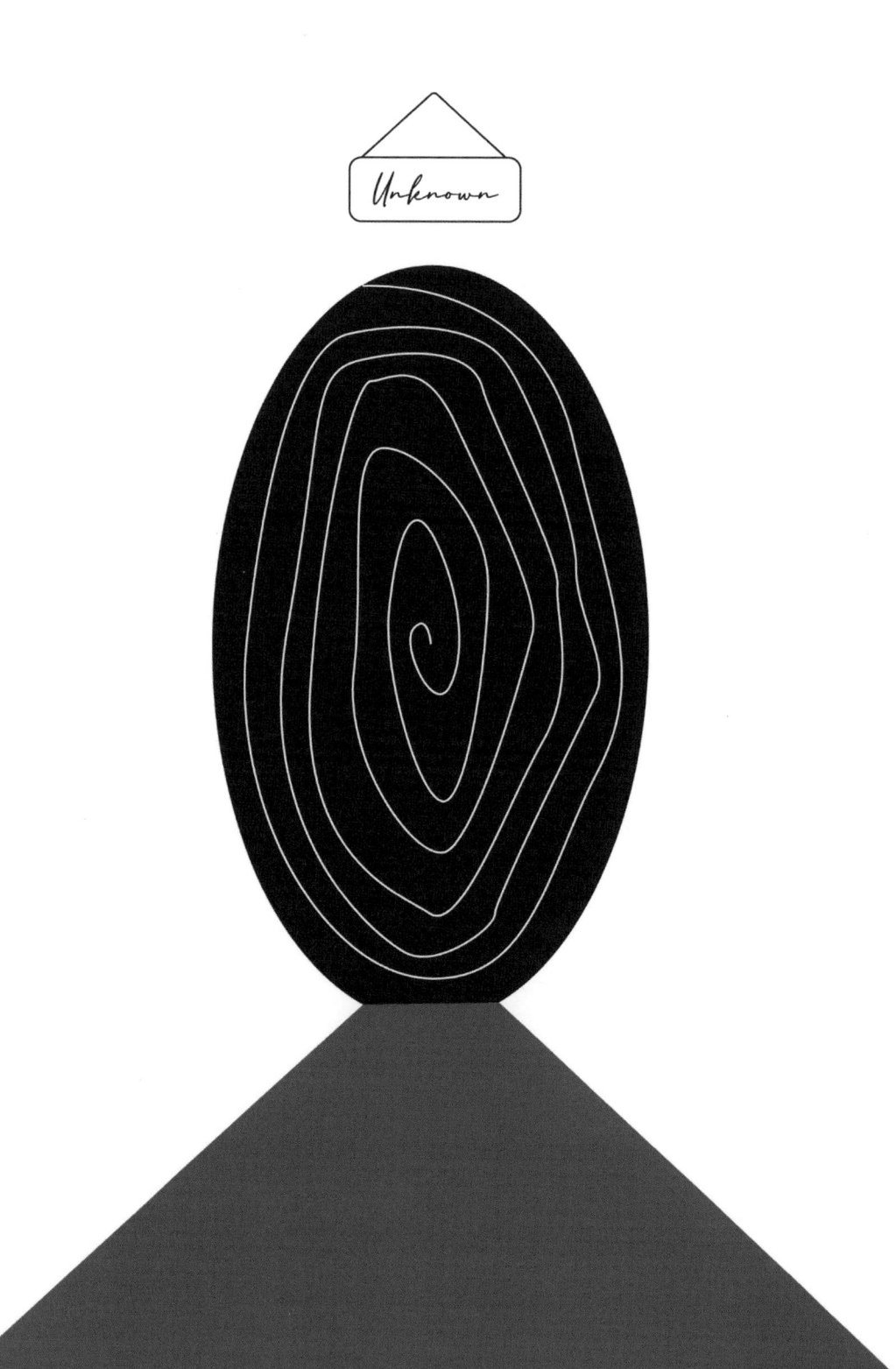

MANTRA #4

I honor the start of my ascension.
By trusting my gut and intuition.
Where it leads I will follow.
What it says I will do.
I am equipped with enough power.
To see this thing through.

*Are you led
by faith or by fear?*

MANTRA #5

Finding the magic in me.
I'm fully capable.

When do you give yourself rest and when do you allow yourself play?

GROW

It is not enough to just refresh your feed.
You must refresh your mind and plant your own seed.
It is okay to be in the moment.
Step away from the screen.
It is okay to feel emotions.
Laugh, cry and scream.
Release, reset, rest and be kind.
To yourself and to strangers who may not be like-mind.
Give the seed that you plant enough space to grow.
Give it love, give it light, let the nutrients flow.
Trust the process of life, and remember to know.
Growth and comfort cannot coexist.
Change is inevitable; try not to resist.
You are worthy of all the good things that you find.
Know your worth.
Protect your peace.
Refresh your mind.

- Ellesse

MANTRA #6

I receive compassion.
May it be instilled in me.
I receive more love.
May it begin with me.

*In what ways do you show yourself compassion?
Now how do you show others?*

MANTRA #7

Wake up and live.

How will you breathe new life into your day?

Lightning Source UK Ltd.
Milton Keynes UK
UKIC031316210521
384097UK00005B/114